PUZZLE ISLAND

S0-BNR-774

Contents

About this story

This story is about a young pirate called Sam Swashbuckle, his pet parrot, Percy, and their adventures on Puzzle Island.

Sam's new boat

Percy the parrot

Useful equipment

Sam Swashbuckle

Skull and crossbones badge

Sam is a junior pirate. To become a real pirate, he has to find a skull and crossbones badge, like the one shown on the left. The badge is hidden in a chest full of treasure and buried somewhere on Puzzle Island. An exciting trail of clues and puzzles will lead Sam to it.

Treasure chest

Puzzle Island

You will find a puzzle on every double page. See if you can solve them all and help Sam to follow the treasure trail. If you get stuck, you can look at the answers on pages 31 and 32.

The Pirate Kit

On his journey, Sam also collects a pirate kit. One piece of kit is hidden on every double page. See if you can spot the pieces as you go. If you can't find them all, the answers on page 32 should help you. Here you can see the complete pirate kit.

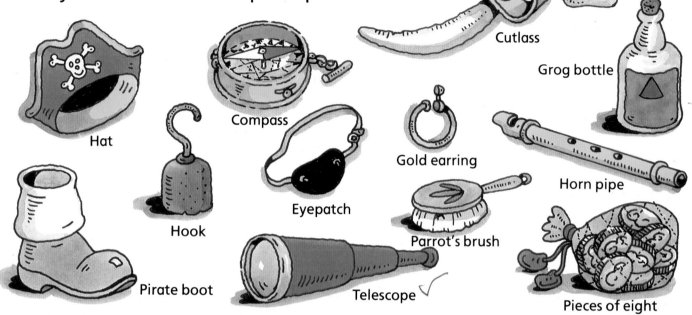

Spare headscarf

Be careful!

Cutlass

Grog bottle

Hat

Compass

Gold earring

Horn pipe

Hook

Eyepatch

Parrot's brush

Pirate boot

Telescope ✓

Pieces of eight

Horatio
Horatio is a sneaky pirate who would love to beat Sam to the treasure on Puzzle Island. He is lurking on almost every double page. Keep your eyes open!

Horatio

HELGA

Horace, Horatio's pet snake

Pink Elephants
Puzzle Island is the home of the only pink elephants in the world. There is at least one pink elephant hiding on every double page. How many can you spot?

Now turn the page to begin the adventure…

3

Sam sets off

Early one morning Sam's adventure began. He was off on his treasure hunt. He waved goodbye to his mum and his dad, his granny and his little sister, and set sail for Puzzle Island in his new red boat.

The sun was shining and the sea was blue. It was a perfect day to look for treasure. But Sam knew he had to keep a special watch out for Horatio, the sneaky pirate. He was sure to be somewhere near.

Can you see Horatio?

4

5

Where is Puzzle Island?

Sam sailed and sailed, until he saw some strange islands ahead. Quickly he checked his sea chart.

"One of them must be Puzzle Island," he cried.

But which one was it? Sam remembered that Puzzle Island was the home of the only pink elephants in the world. If he could spot just one pink elephant, he would have found Puzzle Island.

Can you spot a pink elephant?

Remember to look out for Horatio, and a piece of pirate kit!

The first clue

Sam jumped off his boat, tripped and bumped his head on a large signpost. He was in luck! He had found his first clue.

Sam looked around. He saw lots of paths and lots of arrows. But where was the red and white stripy arrow that would start his treasure hunt?

Can you see it?

FIRST CLUE
Follow the
red and white
stripy arrow

8

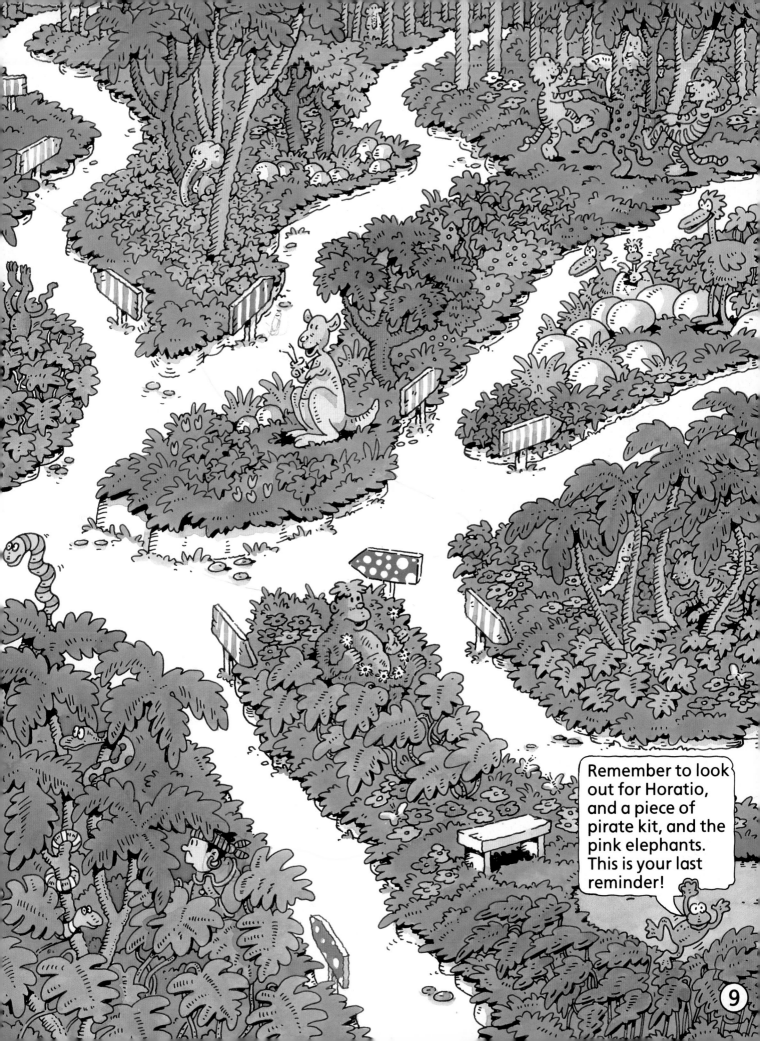

Remember to look
out for Horatio,
and a piece of
pirate kit, and the
pink elephants.
This is your last
reminder!

9

The leafy lake

Sam sped off down the path. He was so excited he almost fell – splash – into a big lake. He tried to run around it, but he couldn't squeeze past the prickly branches.

The lake was covered with lots of giant leaves. Maybe Sam could use them as stepping stones to hop across the lake? But some of the leaves were animals' nests, and some of the leaves had holes in them. He mustn't hop on any of these.

Can you find a way across the lake by hopping from one leaf to another?

NESTING
SEASON
Do not disturb the
baby animals

The safe bridge

Next he came to the edge of a high cliff. He gulped as he looked down. Far below he saw hungry crocodiles and strange animals, bubbling mud and whirling whirlpools.

Ten bridges crossed the gorge. Sam was about to step on to one of them when Percy squawked a warning. Sam looked again and saw that only one bridge was safe to cross.

Do you know which one it is?

Animal spotting

Safe on the other side, Sam saw a strange sight. A man peered down at him from a tall tower.

"I'm on a treasure trail and I don't know where to go next," Sam called. "Can you help me?"

"Yes, if you help me first," said the man. "I've spotted all the animals in my animal spotting book except for a lion, a tiger, a giraffe, a monkey, a snake and a spotty dog. Find me the animals and I'll show you the trail."

Can you spot all the animals?

The volcano maze

The old man told Sam to go to the red flag at the top of the volcano. There he would find something very useful. Sam looked at the maze of paths ahead of him. Would he ever make his way through them?

Can you find your way through the maze to the red flag at the top of the volcano?

Spot the difference

Sam followed the steep, winding path to the top of the volcano. There in the middle of the crater was a big silver key. It looked very useful, so Sam picked it up. Tied to it was a label which told him to go to the orchard. He put the key in his bag and set off at once.

When he reached the orchard, Sam thought he heard noises behind him. Was he being followed? Slowly he looked over his shoulder, but there was no one there.

"I hope I don't bump into Horatio," he shivered.

Suddenly there was a loud cracking noise. Sam spun around. How strange. He was sure there was someone else in the orchard, and several things looked different.

Can you spot the differences between the two pictures?

Find the twins

All of a sudden, Horatio leapt out from behind a tree. But before he could net poor Sam, he was startled by the sound of splashing and shouting. Nearby, children were playing on the beach.

   "Which way to the treasure?" Horatio asked them gruffly.

   Horatio looked very puzzled at the answers, but Sam smiled. He knew the way now.

Where should Sam go next?

Pyramid puzzle

Horatio sped off at once – towards the snake pit! Sam waited until he was out of sight and then ran to the pyramids. There were three of them, one yellow, one red and one blue.

Nailed to some trees, Sam saw four pieces of paper. Quickly he pulled them off and unrolled them. They were four maps of the area. But only one of them was right. This was the map that showed Sam where he would find the next clue.

You can see the maps on the next page. Which is the right map? Where is the next clue?

X marks the spot where the next clue is hidden.

Locked out!

There was a spiked wall all around the blue pyramid. It was much too high for Sam to climb, and the heavy gate was locked with a big padlock. Sam wondered what to do next. Was this the end of the trail?

Suddenly he had a brainwave. There was something in his back pack that would open the gate. Quickly he emptied his bag on the ground.

What can Sam use to open the gate?

The pirate's den

The lock opened with a click. Sam climbed the steps to a door in the pyramid and slowly pushed it open. He found himself in a pirate's den filled with all sorts of strange things.

There were six closed doors inside the den, and on each door there was a message and a picture. Five of the pictures showed places Sam had already been to on his journey around the island. But there was one picture he didn't recognize. This was where he had to go to next.

Which door should Sam go through?

"This way to the"

"This way to the"

POP

Spies at the waterfall

Sam opened the door. He ran down the steps on the other side, through a door in the spiked wall he hadn't seen before, and along a path to the waterfall. On the ground was a cross. Was the treasure buried here?

Quickly he pulled out his spade and began to dig. Just then he heard rustling noises all around him. He was being watched, but he wasn't afraid. He knew the spies were friendly, because he had seen them all before.
How many people do you recognize?

The wonderful treasure!

Sam's spade hit something hard. It was the treasure chest! His friends cheered as Sam puffed and panted and heaved the heavy chest out of the ground. He opened the lid and gasped. Inside was the most wonderful treasure Sam had ever seen. There were glittering jewels and chocolate money, amazing toys and lots of toffees. Then Sam spotted the most important treasure of all. He was a real pirate at last!

Can you see what Sam has spotted?

Hooray!

Sweets

Punk Wig

Answers

Pages 4-5   Sam sets off

Here is Horatio.

Pages 6-7   Where is Puzzle Island?

Here is the pink elephant.

This is Puzzle Island.

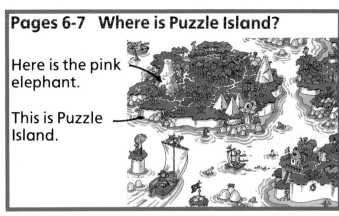

Pages 8-9
The first clue
Here is the red and white stripy arrow.

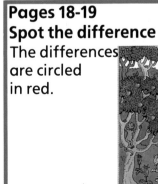

Pages 10-11
The leafy lake
The way across the lake is marked in red.

Pages 12-13
The safe bridge
This is the safe bridge.

Pages 14-15   Animal spotting
The animals are circled in red.

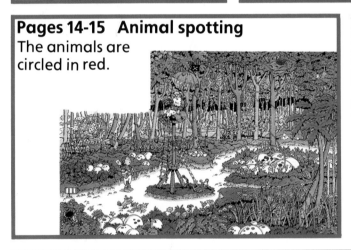

Pages 16-17   The volcano maze
The way to the red flag is marked in red.

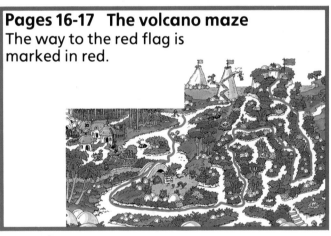

Pages 18-19
Spot the difference
The differences are circled in red.

Pages 20-21
Find the twins
These are the identical twins.

**Pages 22-23
Pyramid puzzle**
This is the right map. The next clue is in the blue pyramid.

**Pages 24-25
Locked out!**
Sam can use the key he found on the volcano.

**Pages 26-27
The pirate's den**
Sam should go through this door.

Pages 28-29 Spies at the waterfall
You don't need an answer to this! Look back through the story and see if you can spot all the characters.

Page 30 The wonderful treasure!
Sam has spotted the skull and crossbones badge. Now he is a real pirate.

Did you spot everything?

Pink Elephants

Pirate Kit

Horatio

The chart below shows you how many pink elephants are hiding on each double page. You can also find out which piece of Sam's pirate kit is hidden on which double page.

Did you remember to look out for Horatio? He may be a sneaky pirate, but he's not as good at hiding as he thinks he is. Look back through the story again and see if you can find him.

Pages	Pink Elephants	Pirate Kit
4-5	Two	Boot
6-7	One	Grog bottle
8-9	Six	Telescope
10-11	Two	Earring
12-13	Two	Spare headscarf
14-15	Three	Hook
16-17	Three	Hornpipe
18-19	One	Compass
20-21	Two	Eyepatch
22-23	Three	Pieces of eight
24-25	Three	Parrot brush
26-27	Two	Cutlass
28-29	Two	Hat
30	Two	

The wonderful treasure
Sam was very happy to find the treasure. He shared it fairly with all his new Puzzle Island friends, but he remembered to save something for his little sister. Even Horatio got a present, and he was so surprised he managed to say thank you!

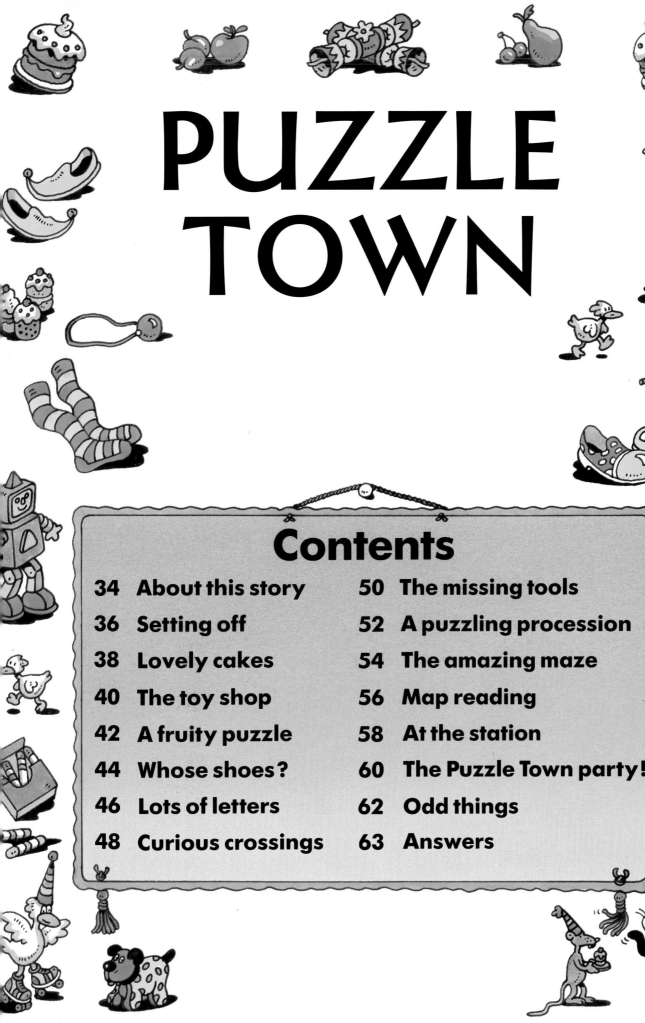

PUZZLE TOWN

Contents

About this story

There's a fancy dress party in Puzzle Town today. Katy and Tim are invited, but they don't know where to find the party.

An exciting trail of clues and puzzles on every double page will lead them to it. See if you can solve them all and help Katy and Tim on their way. If you get stuck you can look at the answers on pages 63 and 64.

Puzzle Town

Tim

Katy

Fancy dress

Here are Katy's and Tim's fancy dress outfits. One piece is hiding on every double page. If you can't spot them all, the answers on page 64 should help you. Can you guess what Katy and Tim are going as?

Face paints

Joke flower

Big shoes

Hat

Cloak

Funny wig

Spell book

Slippers

Red nose

Striped socks

Wand

Magic kitten

Party clues

On some pages there are special party clues, like this one. They will help you find the party, so look out for them.

The party pixie

Party pixie

This is the party pixie. He is in charge of the Puzzle Town party. He helps Katy and Tim on the trail by giving them some important instructions to follow. Keep your eyes peeled.

Odd things

Puzzle Town is a very strange place. If you look very carefully, you will see a lot of odd things. See how many you can spot on every double page.

Boat

Balloon thief

Someone has stolen the Puzzle Town party balloons. The thief is hiding on every double page. Can you spot the balloons he has taken?

Setting off

The day of the Puzzle Town party was sunny and bright. Katy and Tim set off on their trail. In their hands they held a letter from the party pixie.

"First let's work out which Puzzle Town shops we need to go to," said Tim, looking at the letter. "The quicker we do, the quicker we'll find the party."

Which shops must Tim and Katy go to? Can you spot them?

Dear Katy and Tim,
Before you set off on the trail of the Puzzle Town party, here are a few things you must do.
Love from the Party Pixie x x x

Buy some cakes for the party

Get some party hats

Buy party fruit

Collect Katy's new shoes

Post letters

P.S. There are clues along the way and an invitation at the end of the trail. Good luck!

Butcher

Baker's Shop

Lovely cakes

Katy and Tim raced off to the bakers. Here they found some of the most delicious looking cakes they had ever seen. There were gingerbread men and chocolate logs, banana muffins and sugar mice. Katy licked her lips. Which cakes should they take to the party?

Suddenly Tim spotted a big notice. On it was a special message from the party pixie. It told them exactly which cakes to choose.

Can you find the party cakes?

Katy and Tim, please bring these cakes to the party.

1 of these

2 of these

3 of these

2 of these

yum yum

Fish cakes

Sausages

You will find the party next to three tall trees.

The toy shop

Next Katy and Tim headed for the toy shop. Here they found Mr Tedd, the owner, puzzling over a chart pinned to the counter.

"The party pixie has told me to wear one of these four costumes to the Puzzle Town party," Mr Tedd explained, pointing to the poster. "I'll work out which one by finding the only toy in my shop that matches one of these pictures. But is it the king, the ghost, the detective or the cowboy?"

Which costume will Mr Tedd wear to the party?

Pickled Onions

Marbles

Hats

Scooter

Hula Hoops

Super Scooter

King Ghost Detective Cowboy

The party is beside a bridge.

41

A fruity puzzle

At the fruit and vegetable shop Katy and Tim looked at all the delicious things and wondered what to choose. Then Katy spotted a blackboard. It was another special message. Katy and Tim read it carefully. Now they knew exactly what fruit to buy. But there was a catch - every fruit had to be different.

What fruit should Tim and Katy choose?

The party is under a big clock.

Oranges

Katy and Tim
Please choose

3 green fruits
4 red fruits
2 yellow fruits
2 orange fruits

Remember - NO two fruits must be the same.

Apple Tree

Doughnut Tree

42

43

Whose shoes?

With the fruit in their bags, Tim and Katy skipped off to collect Katy's new sandals from the shoe shop. But the shop was in a dreadful mess, and none of the customers had any shoes on at all.

"I'll fetch your sandals in a minute, Katy," said Clive, the assistant. "But first I must find shoes for all these people."

Can you help Clive match the customers with their shoes?

45

Lots of letters

The Post Office was the last place on their list. Here Katy and Tim found three letter boxes, each for a different type of mail. Zippy mail was for urgent letters, Snail mail was for letters that weren't very important and Air mail was for letters going to another country. Tim and Katy read the Post Office notice board and looked at the stamps on their letters. They soon worked out what they had to do.

Which letters should go into which letter boxes?

Look carefully at your stamps.
Please put all your letters into the right letter boxes.

Zippy mail = 10 Puzzle Pennies

Snail mail = 5 Puzzle Pennies

Air mail = 15 Puzzle Pennies

Zippy mail only = 10PP

PARCEL POST

Mrs Ellie Phant. ABROAD.

Zippy

Curious crossings

Now their errands were done, but Tim and Katy still hadn't found the party. Then Tim had a brainwave. They would ask their friend Molly, the mechanic at the Puzzle Town garage, what to do next. She knew everything.

Outside the Post Office, Katy and Tim saw they had to cross lots of roads to reach the garage. They knew the Puzzle Town Road Code - only cross at the striped crossings. But some of the crossings were blocked, so they couldn't cross at these.

Can you find a safe route to the garage using the clear crossings only?

Pirates rule

Treasure for ALL!

Horatio is innocent

Molly's Garage

The missing tool kit

At the garage, Katy and Tim found Molly looking for her lost tools. She had lots of Puzzle Town cars to mend.

"I'll help you on your way to the party, if you two help me find my missing tools," said Molly. "I've lost a screwdriver, a saw, a hammer, a light, a very big nail and my new red cleaning cloth."

Katy and Tim looked around the messy garage. It certainly wasn't going to be an easy job.

Can you find Molly's lost tools?

50

A puzzling procession

Molly smiled mysteriously. She told the children to follow the group with the most legs in the Puzzle Town procession. There were four groups to choose from - the jolly rollerskaters, the silly skateboards, the prancing ponies and the unusual unicyclists.

Katy and Tim were wondering what she meant, when suddenly they heard laughter and cheering. Racing outside they saw, to their surprise, a strange procession of people and animals. But which was the group with most legs? Then Tim gave a shout. He knew who to follow.

Which group should Tim and Katy follow?

e amazing maze

prancing ponies led Katy and Tim to the
zzle Town park. When they told the children
here was something for them in the middle of the
maze, Katy and Tim groaned. The maze was so
big and twisty. Would they ever find their way to
the middle, and out again?

Can you find the way to the middle of the maze?

Map reading

In the middle of the maze, Katy and Tim found an envelope addressed to them. Inside was their party invitation and a message from the party pixie, listing the five clues they had already found. There was also a map, showing the other side of Puzzle Town.

"Now we can find the party," said Katy.

Look at all the clues again. Then look at the map. Where is the party being held?

Katy and Tim are invited to the Puzzle Town party today at 3pm.

You will find the party next to three tall trees.

The party is beside a bridge.

The party is under a big clock.

The party is in a street that begins with an 'S'.

The party is outside a brown building. (It doesn't look like this one).

The above five clues will help you find the Puzzle Town party on the map.

Dear Katy and Tim,
Before you go to the Puzzle Town party, please
collect the party guests from Puzzle Town Station.
Love from the Party Pixie ×××

Strange Street

Station

Station Road

Riddle Row

Silly Street

Loony Lane

Magic Roundabout

Pudding Hill

Odd Avenue

Mystery Road

Pixie Place

Never End

Slimy Street

Sweet Street

Sticky Street

At the station

At last Katy and Tim knew where the party was. But first they had to rush to Puzzle Town station.

   "The party guests have arrived," called Joe the guard. "They're waiting for you on the party train."

   "Which one is it?" asked Katy.

   "It has a green engine, or is it blue? I know it's got spots and is driven by engineer Emma," Joe said.

Can you find the Puzzle Town party train?

Puzzle Town Station

59

The Puzzle Town party!

Katy and Tim led the way to the Puzzle Town party, followed by all their new friends. And what a party it was! There were cakes and clowns, jugglers and jellies, bubbles and balloons. Katy and Tim saw lots of familiar faces. Even the mysterious balloon thief was there. As for the party pixie, well he was already planning next year's Puzzle Town party.

How many party guests have you seen before? Can you spot the balloon thief?

Odd things

Did you spot all the odd things going on in Puzzle Town? If not, go back and have another look. If you can't find them, here's a list of all the things Katy and Tim saw on their adventure.

Pages	Odd things
36-37	Sea monster, tiger on a swing, twisty chimney, broken broom handle, duck in boots, the flower shop door is in a strange place!
38-39	Broken chair leg, upside-down teapot spout, a polar bear eating a biscuit, sausages hanging from roof.
40-41	Pickled onions, web-footed doll, aliens, boy with one bare foot.
42-43	Giant legs at crossing, broken trolley handle, duck, tree trunk, doughnut tree.
44-45	Chicks in a box, shoe box full of bananas, child with boot on head, duck in boots.
46-47	Alien photos, parcelled elephant, parcelled snake.
48-49	Ballet-dancing hippo, giraffe in car, monster in pond.
50-51	Dog mechanic, three-wheeled car, snake hose, flowers in exhaust.
52-53	Giraffe in house, feet in roof, dog taking man for a walk.
54-55	Person dressed for winter, upside-down boots, plug in hedge, bird wearing hat, man with three legs.
56-57	Animal with sunglasses, silly street names.
58-59	Tiger dressed as person, lady with upside-down umbrella, strange creatures, ice-skater, firebucket, man in skirt, boat sign.
60-61	What a strange party!

Answers

Pages 36-37
Setting off

These are the shops that Katy and Tim should go to.

Post Office — letters.

Shoe shop — shoes.

Fruit and vegetable shop — fruit.

Bakers — cakes.

Toy shop — party hats.

Pages 38-39
Lovely cakes

The cakes are circled in red.

Pages 40-41 The toy shop

The ghost is the only toy that appears in the shop and on the chart. So Mr Tedd must choose the ghost costume.

Pages 42-43 A fruity puzzle

You could choose several different combinations of fruit. But Katy and Tim chose these:
Green — apple, grape, lime; Red — cherry, plum, strawberry, rhubarb; Yellow — lemon, banana; Orange — peach, orange.

Pages 44-45
Whose shoes?

You can find the shoes and the feet they fit by matching the coloured circles shown here.

Pages 46-47
Lots of letters

Zippy mail

Zippy mail

Snail mail

Snail mail

Air mail

Zippy mail

Pages 48-49 Curious crossings

The route across the clear crossings is marked in red.

Pages 50-51
The missing tools

Molly's missing tools are circled in red.

63

Pages 52-53
A puzzling procession

The prancing ponies are the group with the most legs in the procession.

Pages 54-55
The amazing maze

The way through the maze is marked in red.

Pages 56-57
Map reading

This is the place where the party is being held. It is the only place on the map that matches all the clues.

Pages 58-59
At the station

This is the Puzzle Town party train.

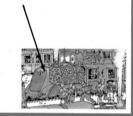

Pages 60-61
The Puzzle Town party!

This is the balloon thief.

Look back through the story and see if you can spot all the people who are now at the party.

Did you spot everything?
Fancy dress

The chart below shows you which piece of either Katy's or Tim's fancy dress costume is hidden on which double page. Katy's costume is a wizard, and Tim's is a clown.

Pages	Fancy dress
36-37	Magic kitten
38-39	Spell book
40-41	Joke flower
42-43	Wand
44-45	Striped socks
46-47	Slippers
48-49	Red nose
50-51	Cloak
52-53	Big shoes
54-55	Hat
56-57	Face paints
58-59	Funny wig

Balloon thief

Did you remember to look out for that naughty balloon thief? At least he brought the balloons to the party in the end!

Next year's party . . .

The party pixie is already looking forward to next year's Puzzle Town party. He is planning all sorts of puzzles and wonderful surprises. Katy and Tim are very excited about the plans for next year's party too, but they have a special request. Next year, they'd like to get their invitation through the mail, like everyone else.

PUZZLE FARM

Contents

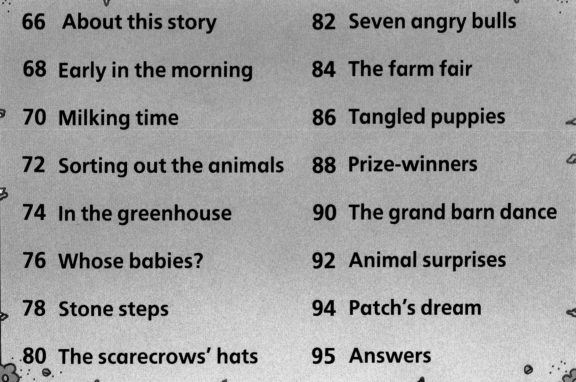

About this story

This story is about Beth and Harry and their adventures on Puzzle Farm.

Puzzle Farm

We will be back in time for the fair!

Beth

Harry

Farmhands

Tilly

Tilly, the Puzzle Farmer, and all her farm helpers have gone on a day trip to Puzzle Island. Beth and Harry are in charge of Puzzle Farm for the day. They have a lot to do as it's the farm fair in the afternoon. Some of their friends from nearby Puzzle Town have come to help them out.

Puzzle Town friends

You will find a puzzle on every double page. See if you can solve them all and help Beth, Harry and the Puzzle Town people get everything ready for the fair. If you get stuck, you can look at the answers on pages 95 and 96.

The musical instruments

Tilly and her helpers have planned a surprise for after the fair. For this they will need their musical instruments. One instrument is hidden on almost every double page. Here you can see them all.

cymbals

fiddle

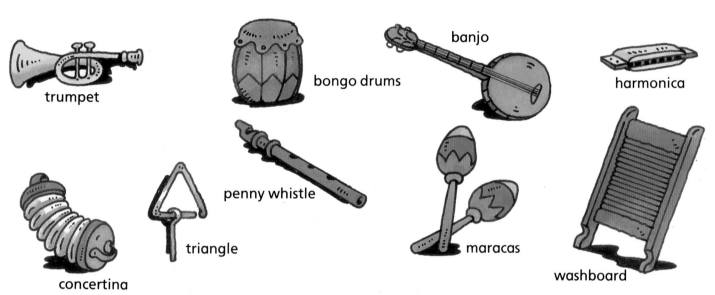

trumpet

bongo drums

banjo

harmonica

penny whistle

concertina

triangle

maracas

washboard

Patch

Patch is the farm puppy. Beth and Harry want to enter him in the puppy competition. But Patch has other ideas. He is hiding on every double page.

Can you spot him?

Purple puzzle mice

Puzzle Farm is the home of the only purple puzzle mice in the world. There is at least one mouse hiding on every double page. Keep your eyes open!

Early in the morning

On the day of the fair, Harry and Beth woke up early. There was a lot to do on Puzzle Farm.

First they had to feed the pony, the pig, the chicken, the duck and the rabbit. These were the animals that lived in the farmyard. But there was no sign of them. And where was Patch, the naughty farm puppy? Beth and Harry had to keep a special eye out for him.

Can you find all the farmyard animals?

Milking time

Beth and Harry fed the farmyard animals and then followed Patch's pawprints to the milking shed. Here they found Clive from Puzzle Town.

"I have to milk these cows," he wailed. "But I can't put them in the right milking stalls because I don't know their names."

"That's easy," said Beth. "Each cow looks like her name."

Can you see where each cow should go?

BIG SPOTS SHAGGY BELLE SOCKS

71

Sorting out the animals

Outside the milking shed, Harry and Beth heard noises coming from the next field. They raced over and saw Mr Stamp the postman. He was looking at lots of different animals.

"Tilly told me to divide these animals into three groups ready for the fair," he said. "There's the spotty group, the feathered creatures and the animals with horns. But I can't work out which animals belong in which group."

Can you?

73

In the greenhouse

Their next stop was the greenhouse. Tilly had given Harry and Beth special instructions to pick five flowers for the farm fair. She didn't mind what they looked like, as long as each flower was a different shape and a different shade.

Can you find five different flowers?

Whose babies?

In the field behind the greenhouse, Harry and Beth saw all kinds of animals wandering about. In the middle of them stood Mrs Bagel, the baker, scratching her head.

"These mother animals have lost their babies," she said. "I know the babies look just like their mothers, but I still can't match them up."

Can you match the baby animals with their mothers?

e steps

...asks were nearly finished when Beth ...mbered Tilly's best hat. It had been lent to one of the scarecrows and Harry and Beth had to find it in time for the fair.

The scarecrows were in a far away field surrounded by high walls. The only way through was the stone steps. But some of the steps weren't safe to climb and some were blocked.

Can you find a way across the fields to the scarecrows?

The scarecrows' hats

Beth and Harry arrived, puffing and panting at the field of scarecrows. There was a surprise waiting for them. All the scarecrows were wearing hats! Which one was Tilly's? Then Harry remembered that Tilly's hat was mostly red, and the flowers on it weren't blue or green. It should be easy to find.

Which is Tilly's hat?

Seven angry bulls

In the next field, Mr Tedd the toy shop man, was struggling to control seven angry bulls.

"I must keep these bullies apart," he cried. "But they all have to stay in this field. I've got these three special anti-bull poles to separate them. I've put one pole down, and now I don't know where the other two should go.

Can you fit the other two poles so that each bull is in a separate part of the field?

The farm fair

At last Beth and Harry finished all their tasks. Excitedly they set off for the fair. At the entrance they found Joe, the station master, looking very worried.

"The fair is about to start," he said. "My job was to meet Tilly. She's opening the fair. But she's not here and we can't start without her."

Can you see Tilly at the fair?

PONY RACE

FATTEST HEN CONTEST

LOST PETS

Smelliest Flower Contest

Prettiest Piggy

FRUIT STALL

WELCOME TO THE PUZZLE FARM FAIR

LOG SAWING

Tangled puppies

Beth and Harry breathed a sigh of relief. The fair had begun! Then they remembered the puppy competition. They raced to the main show ring, but Patch was nowhere to be seen. Inside the ring, the competition had begun. It was very confusing. Each contestant had two puppies, but the leads were all tangled up, and no one knew whose puppies were whose.

Can you untangle the leads and find out which puppies belong to which child?

Prize-winners

At five o'clock everyone went to the judges' tent for the prize giving ceremony. But the prize-winners' list was lost. Now no one knew who should win which prize, or what competition they had entered. Beth and Harry looked at the prize-winners – the horse, the hen, the flowers, the cake and the pig. Then they thought back to all they had seen at the fair that day. Soon they knew which prize each had won.

Can you match the prizes to the winners?

The grand barn dance

But the fun wasn't over yet. That night, to celebrate the fair, there was a grand barn dance at Puzzle Farm. All the farm hands were back from their holiday. They played their instruments loudly as everyone danced the farmyard fling. But Mabel and Doris Green from the fruit and vegetable shop weren't smiling. They needed six red apples to finish making the fizzy farmyard fruit punch, and they couldn't see them anywhere.

Can you find the six red apples?

Animal surprises

When the music stopped, Harry and Beth heard another sound in the distance. They tiptoed quietly out into the dark night. The noise was getting louder and it came from the animal shed. Creeping nearer, they peered in through the window and saw a strange sight. The animals were having their very own barn dance! And at last Beth and Harry had found Patch.

How many animals have you seen before? Where is Patch?